Copyright © 2024 by Emma Walker.

All rights reserved. No part of this book may be used or reproduced in any form whatsoever without written permission except in the case of brief quotations in critical articles or reviews.

ISBN - Paperback: 978-1-06702-495-6

There was the before loss me and my before loss life.
For all that has changed, its all because of love.

Unsure

I'm unsure of who I am,
What I need,
What I should do,
And who'll still be there when I find the new me.

Your Person

Some people just are your world,
Your person,
Your safety,
Your third ear,
Your shoulder,
Your rationality during emotional times,
Your trust,
Your companion,
Your best friend,
For me, this was you mum.

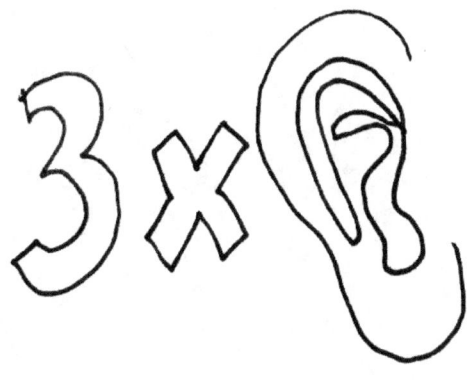

Lost

I'm lost without you now.
The kind of lost where I can't look forward,
Can't go back,
I'm frozen on the spot.

Legs like lead,
Mind all bent,
And my heart yearns for you to come back.

Thank you

For everything,
For your constant love,
For the lessons you taught me,
For giving your heart and soul.

You've given me strength,
You've taught me compassion,
I'm so incredibly proud to call you,
My mum.

Endless

Like a fire with an endless flame,
My love for you will always remain,
It burns so bright,
It runs so deep,
It was you who showed me how endless love can be.

Unfair

Why can life be so unfair,
People get taken away,
Gone from your life,
Taken far too soon,
Transcending you to the hardest moments and impossible goodbyes.

Ones that shouldn't happen,
Those you'll never be ready for,
No matter how many more moments are shared.

The impossibility of death,
Of loss,
Of grief,
Of futures we didn't get to have.

Flower shops

I look for your favourites,
And I want to buy you the whole shop,
But I want to do that with you still here,
I want to shower you with love.

I know your favourite colours,
The combinations you preferred.
I know what type you would order for others,
You were such a generous soul.

Café

If I could visit one more with you,
If I could order your favourite drink,
I would make it last forever,
And stare at you so proudly.

Trivial

I don't have time for trivial things,
Patience, not a cloak I can continue to wear.

The trivial,
The material,
Feels like its everywhere,
Flooding through society,
Taking up too much space.

You didn't dabble in any nonsense,
Always so real,
So genuine,
And so wholeseome.

Now, seeing the trivial around me since you've been gone,
It tears at my heart so much,
I just want you back.

Anniversaries

Do I treasure the ones we had together,
Or pretend the day hasn't come.

Do I hide away from society,
It feels like too much to bear.

Shall I just wing it on the day?
That feels like our approach,
How we would navigate this together.

Now that you're not here,
These days much harder,
More impossible to comprehend,
But I will channel the inspiration you've imparted,
And do my best to make you proud.

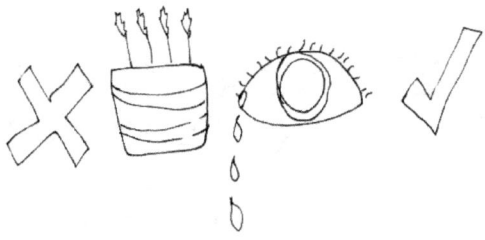

Filter

I filter out conversations,
Visuals and reminders,
So many everyday.

It's not until you've lost someone so close,
That you realise the volume of triggers in everyday life.
They come thick and fast,
Like a back up of traffic at a green light.

Some days I can filter more,
Other days much less,
Its moments, conversations, people and songs
Whereever I look,
Reminders, they're everywhere.

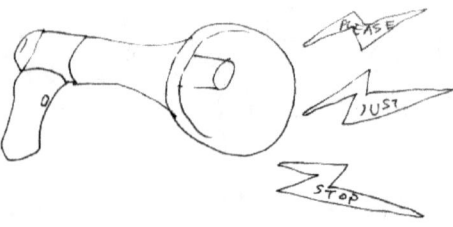

Connected

My love to you,
A bond that will never be broken,
The most robust of bridges,
Each day growing stronger,
With each memory shared together,
I'm holding them so close,
And will be sure to treasure them forever.

Full time

I want to do all the things we did together,
And revisit those you did alone.

I want to commemorate you with so many actions, words, roadtrips and moments, so much so that I wish I wish honouring you could be my full-time job.

OCCUPATION: GRIEVING

Scurried off

Just days have gone by,
But the days have gotten harder,
The people much quieter,
All those around have gone back to their own lives.

I just hope they peer out the window from time to time,
Parting their curtains as they look out.

To show me they're here,
To show me they've stayed,
And that when I'm ready,
They'll come on back out.

Secondary

When I think of loss,
The peak of this is you,
There's other things,
Including myself,
The old me no longer exists.

What does not compare is everything to you,
The absence felt since you left the earth,
Nothing will ever be the same.

Bereavement is permanent as far as I'm concerned,
There is no timeframe.
It's a journey fraught with change,
Entwined with further loss and pain,
One I never wanted to take.

The truth

How we know true love is when we lose this person,
What we are left with is memories,
Someone to honour so dearly,
Whilst our heart beats on,
But forever hurting.

Frozen

If I could decide,
On plans,
Even just one,
It involves dealing with the future,
But the truth is in fact,
I remain back in the past.

No mirrors here

There's no two the same,
When it comes to grief,

The way each of us react,
What we need and what may help,
A mystery to those around,
And moreso to the one who is grieving,
For they have lost themselves.

Its not just their loved one whose gone,
Its everything they have known.

The basics

I can do some basic things,
I do them everyday but they don't come with ease,
My capacity just a slither of what it used to be.

Truth

What's truer than true is my love for you.
One that will never stop,
Even though your time on earth has ended,
I'll carry you with me for the rest of my life.

Appreciation

A society that denies one to take their time,
Everyone is in a rush.

I refuse to pick up the pace,
For with grief there is no timeframe.

Occasionally I feel the pressure,
Often self imposed.

Other times its different things,
Different words,
Or other stressors,
My answer remains the same,
Please don't make me rush.

Priorities

It's the people, not the places,
And certainly not the things.

What loss has taught me is just how much love there truly is to give.

Now that you're gone,
The love boils over like its an overflowing pot.

My heart now raging hot,
A burning flame,
Unwavering pain,
A constant ache for all that its lost.

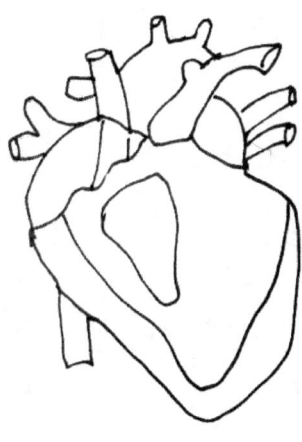

Hand in hand

I hold out my hand,
To my undeniable companion,
Its me and my grief these days.

We go everywhere together,
Including the routine and mundane.

Its my most constant friend, we don't spend time apart.
This grief pal I have represents my love for you and it will always have space in my heart.

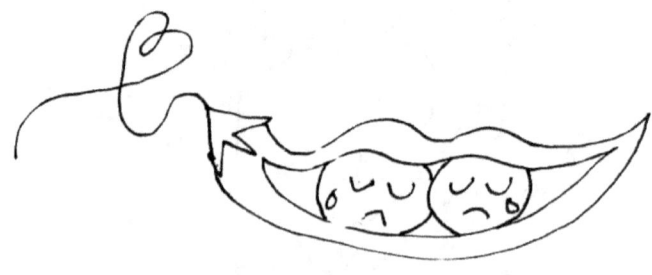

Hope

When hope is lost,
When its left your sight,
Just remember how far you've come.

From where you were,
To where you are now,
That's not to be forgotten,
But admired.

You have fight in you,
You have spirit and strength,
And a fire in your soul.

Keep going for them,
Keep going for you,
And speak of them along your way.

Goodbyes

Its the most painful goodbyes,
The agonising farewells,
The impossible moments,
The tragic loss of tomorrows.

These bring grief,
They show love,
They cause sorrow,
And by gosh they are hard to swallow.

Projections

Grief pushes us to our most stressed
-out state of being,
Like a deer in headllights,
That ready for a fight, running on
adrenaline contant feeling.

If you can do one thing today,
Recognise your fragility,
Show up for yourself,
Give yourself permission to just be
yourself and to grieve.

Maybe

On the days you are so overwhelmed,
Its like you've landed on mars.

You can't reach the outer world,
There's no grasp in sight,
To a sense of functionality,
To a realm where you can cope.

These days are full of learning and falls with no soft landing,
And lessons that reveal just how much inner strength you hold.

You have it within you,
More than you think,
To have your own back,
To rely on your instincts.

Love

For what love teaches us there's no denying,
Its everything,
Or at least its all that matters.

When we lose our loved ones,
When they leave this earth,
There goes our innocense,
And our ability to find hope.

It will come back,
We will find a way,
To carry their strength,
To show them we will be ok.

Butterfly

With fragile wings,
Not landing for long,
Sensitive to the wind,
To other insects,
and to the stimuli around.

Often travelling solo,
Paving its own path,
Finding its flowers,
And where it needs to land.

Maybe we can learn from these innocent creatures,
That every journey of grief is unique.

We can find our own way,
And what we truly need,
To navigate such pain,
And meet our daily needs.

Moon phase

Phases and stages,
No two the same,
Each night a different look,
A different angle,
A different shade.

When we look up at the moon,
At the stars high in the sky,
We can speak to the moving clouds,
As as we sit there and think of our loved ones.

As we can show up like the moon,
Different each day,
All the stages that we go through,
Not linear,
But unique.

Harsh

What really is too harsh is that you had to go,
To leave earth,
I can't come to terms with this,
My heart keeps screaming "NO".

I haven't felt at ease,
Since our parting,
Our goodbye.

I don't think there is anything that I need,
Or that would even help.

The very thing I need is you and nothing can bring you back,
So, I will keep sending you love and look for signs you're nearby,
Up high in those fluffy white clouds.

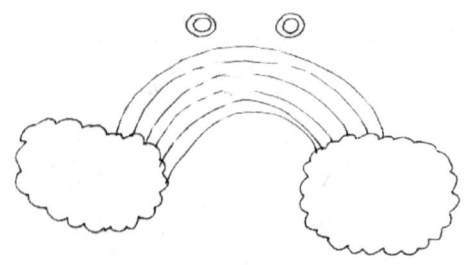

No thanks

I don't want your silver linings,
Or to be forced to sip from your positive cup.
I just need to be with my feelings,
And for you to hold space,
That is all that I ask.

Banter

Banter away,
But to join I may not.

Its too hard to gossip,
To arrive at this conversation took more than a lot.
Social energy is lacking,
Conversation doesn't flow.

I'm here with my thoughts,
Feeling alone with my loss.

Memories

Memories of the past,
Will remain in my grasp,
I will hold them so tightly,
They will not stray far.

Everything

Unrecognisable springs to mind,
Relating to everything I touch and see,
Who I am and where I stand.

It's a change in relationships,
A change in myself,
Upheaval of routine,
As if I've fallen hugely off track.

It's a treacherous journey,
Plagued with twists and turns,
Of jolts and tumbles,
And plunging down rabbit holes.

Each day a new measure of hours,
To measure as I go,
Fumbling through each one of them,
But nowhere feels like home.

Realisations

When we say goodbye to a loved one,
The pain can bring us to our knees,
Overcome with emotion,
Swamped by the crash of waves.

Trembling from the pain,
And the impossibility of their passing,
Each day slowly realising that they're not coming back.

Letting yourself be dragged through the tide,
The waves rolling over and over,
As you hang on with all your might.

As they pour over you,
While you pour out whats left of your heart,
You weep for your loved one,
And the future you envisioned you would have.

Midnight skies

Dark and mysterious,
How many others are awake.

Startled from a deep pattern,
Rest feels far away,
Anything truly restorative no longer a part of your day.

Waiting for the day to break,
For the rousing of anxiety,
And the racing pace of your heart.

Ride

Grief is like riding a rollercoaster,
A perpetual one with no brakes.
Your scared of heights,
And petrified,
Screaming for it to stop.
Its stuck on a loop,
Its pathway has no end,
You're learning how to stay on it the best way that you can.

No matter how much time goes by,
The pain continues,
But you know deep down,
These feelings represent so much love.

Reasoning

How does one reason with themselves when nothing makes sense.
The answer to most things in life is to work hard for what you need and want.

When it comes to grief,
You can't bring your loved one back,
No matter what you would do,
And the fact you'd never stop.

Your existence swept away by missing them so much,
Nobody can do or say anything to take the pain away.
You just grind out the moments,
The hours,
The days,
As the clock ticks on you're desperately trying to find your own pathway.

The everyday complex

To be human,
To have such complex thoughts and emotions,
Can result in so much heartbreak.

We know the tomorrows are changed,
The todays spent in pain,
Our pathways ahead have halted,
Never to be the same again.

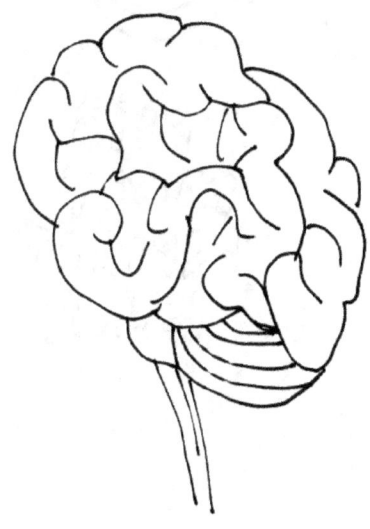

Tear drops

The tears flow so freely down my cheeks,
Endless they are,
Along with them is the infinite love I hold for you so very deep within my heart.

Path

Time moves in its own way,
But its not time that will take this pain away.

This pain is here to stay,
This pain is love,
A forever feeling,
The most forever one I have,
Its entwined within my DNA.

Wounded

The biggest bandaid here on earth wouldn't contain this gaping wound,
Its jagged edges and endless depth growing wider with each passing day.

The wound that grief leaves on the hearts of those left behind.
One that affects the mind, body and soul.

Nightshift

Eyes closed,
Mind wandering,
Drifting off,
Thoughts swirling,
Aching to dream of you,
Stirring through the hours,
Lying there awake,
All the while,
The awareness and connection to the pain.

In the brief moments before I come to realise that every day,
All I want is to see your face,
To hear your voice,
To sit with you and talk,
But you're the very one that I can't have.

Everything

The hardest thing about this,
Is not one thing at all,
It's EVERYTHING.

HOW ART THOU?
NOT OKAY!

Never

My heart will never say goodbye,
It will always belong to you.
This day and everyday forward,
I will think of you.

Hold

Walking hand in hand,
Visiting places we could have gone,
Catching up on everything,
Is where my heart belongs.

There will never be anyone like you,
And knowing you,
Having you in my life,
Even though for a period far too brief,
I am so grateful you were mine.

I love you.

The experience

The waves that feel like hours,
Come crashing down on your whole being,
Throwing you for six,
Like an inflated balloon being let loose in the room.
Out of control and soaring along,
At an uncanny rate of knots.

The grief takes hold and makes you want to scream,
It makes you feel insane,
It makes you realise that you had never really felt pain until this devastating loss.

Questions

What makes the least sense,
Is having to try and do routine and mundane things post loss.

What is cooking and cleaning and hurrying around,
Talking to strangers,
Paying bills and life admin,
When you can't concentrate,
You can't focus,
You can't give the slightest of cares to anything apart from the fact that you want you're loved one back.

Searching

Listening and looking for the right words verbally or on paper,
Trying to find comfort anywhere at any time and trying to ignore the pain caused from those who have turned their back.

```
Steam rolled

Life is a steam roller,
That rolls straight through you with
loss,
It crushes you,
Destroys you,
Leaves you flattened,
Exhausted,
Hurting and battered,
Then turning to roll back around for
plenty more strikes.
```

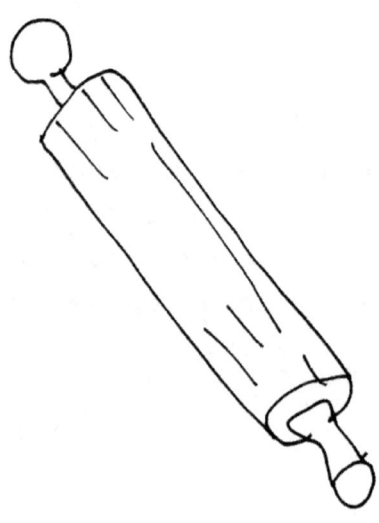

Polite

Let's be real,
Society out here,
Not the warmest place,
To be open with ones feelings,
Ones emotions,
And the stark reality of loss.

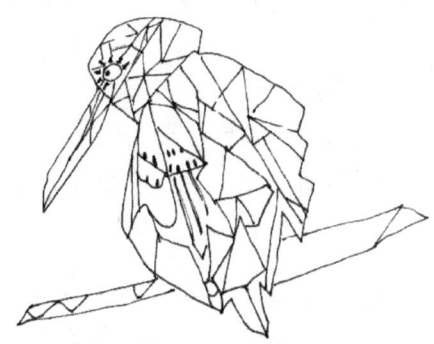

Noise cloud

A reflection of the howl of the wind,
Of the roaring engine of a motorbike,
An uncontrolled spin of a washing machine,
Or the crashing wave on the ocean floor.

Loud noises,
Natures screams,
Manmade bellows,
What I feel constantly inside my mind,
A perpetual need to scream,
To release some of this pain,
That signifies the neverending sorrow.

New

Connecting with someone new,
Those post loss friendships formed,
Those that only know the person you are now that you carry the pain of losing someone you love.

Those are solid friendships,
Ones that you hope to hold onto,
To treasure,
And to cherish.

The people who have shown up in the storms and chaos of your life,
Those are treasured souls,
and a sign of hearts aligned.

The love vine

Some bonds will never break,
Never fracture,
Never tarnish,
Never stretch.

They will hold strong,
Even after loss,
They will always be remembered,
Honoured and cherished.

Like deep seated roots of the strongest tree,
Its roots the love that is forever entwined,
Growing stronger each year,
Filling up all the corners of your heart.

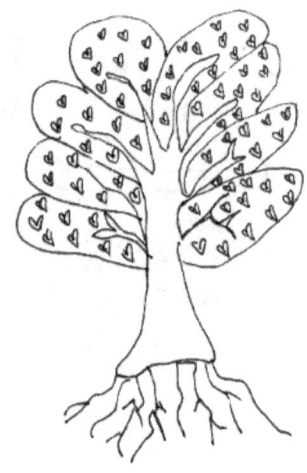

Procrastinating from tasks that feel so soon,
Too hard,
Too rushed,
The problem is they keep feeling that way no matter how much time has passed.

With loss, there's layers of expectations, tasks, behaviours, and difficult conversations.

Painful reminders brought to the surface far to soon,
Moreso than what you feel conditioned to handle.

To get up each day,
To try and remain unbattered by whats spoken,
Whats asked of you,
And whats required.

You say, too soon,
No more, please wait,
Sometimes recognised,
But other times,
The world pushes back and refuses your requests.

Gemstone

Someone that has been with you for all your years,
Your entire existence,
Who knows you far better than anyone else you have met.

That is a goodbye that hurts beyond words,
The very one you want to call,
To cry with,
To hold,
Is the one that you've lost,
An impossible farewell.

Salt wept

The pillows,
The shower,
The bathroom floor,
The soggy sleeves,
The four walls of the car.

Places that have witnessed such vulnerability and sadness,
They've allowed the tears to flow, wiping the moisture from your tear-stained cheeks.

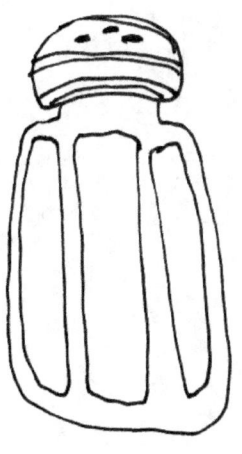

Springboard

Imagine a springboard,
With coils so strong,
A platform so bouncy,
That you could fly up to the clouds
to kiss your loved ones.

www.ingramcontent.com/pod-product-compliance
Lightning Source LLC
Chambersburg PA
CBHW070440010526
44118CB00014B/2127